EYEWITNESS

AFTER DARK

Written by Fiona Waters

Illustrated by Gary Boller

HENDERSON
An imprint of DK Publishing, Inc.

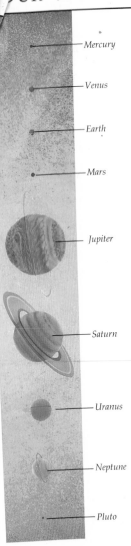

Mercury

Venus

Earth

Mars

Jupiter

Saturn

Uranus

Neptune

Pluto

Everything that exists, including the Earth and the farthest star, is called the *Universe*. Scientists think that it exploded into being anywhere from 1.5 billion years ago to 20 billion years ago! This giant explosion became known as the Big Bang.

WHIRLING AROUND

The Sun, the nine planets that *orbit* (move around) it, and their moons are called the Solar System. The whole thing moves around, together with millions of stars, in a part of space called the *galaxy*.

The planets in our Solar System are called Mercury, Venus, Earth, Mars, Jupiter, Saturn, Uranus, Neptune, and Pluto.

NIGHT AND DAY

The Earth spins on its axis (an imaginary line through its middle), turning once in 24 hours as it orbits the Sun. This rotation gives us night and day. As the Earth rotates into the light of the Sun we have sunrise, and as the Earth continues to rotate away from the light of the Sun we have sunset.

LONG JOURNEY

It takes the Earth 365 and a $^1/_4$ days to circle around the Sun, which is why there are 365 days in a year! The quarter doesn't get lost; every fourth year an extra day is added to February. Since the Earth's orbit is not round but oval, we are closer to the Sun at some times than at others.

The Earth is always tilted at the same angle.

THE MOON

The Moon is the closest thing to Earth – that's why we can see it so clearly. There are lots of other objects in the night sky that are bigger than the Moon, but they look tiny because they are so far away.

MOON MYTHS

In most mythology, the Moon is seen as feminine, but in Europe people used to believe that there was a man in the Moon, put there to make amends for his sins.

When you look at a full Moon it is easy to imagine faces or animal shapes. The Chinese and the Mexicans thought that a hare lived in the Moon.

MOON MAPS

The first map of the Moon was made by the Italian *astronomer* (a scientist who studies the stars and the planets) Galileo, in 1610. In the 19th century, two men named Johann Heinrich Madler and Wilhelm Beer produced amazingly accurate maps. Today, only the areas near the *poles* (the points at the top and the bottom) are as yet unmapped.

ECLIPSES

Every few years you can see a *lunar eclipse*. This is when the Sun, the Earth, and the Moon line up perfectly, and the Earth comes between the Sun and the Moon. The Earth's shadow can be seen crossing the Moon.

An eclipse of the Moon – when it passes through shadow cast by the Earth

As the Moon moves out of the light of the Sun, more and more of it is engulfed in shadow. Sometimes a strange reddish glow is still visible.

A lunar eclipse can be seen from only half the world at a time.

COLUMBUS THE MAGICIAN

Eclipses can be forecast very accurately. In 1504, the explorer and navigator Christopher Columbus was shipwrecked in Jamaica and found that the islanders were not very welcoming. By predicting an eclipse on February 29, he was able to wow them and prove that he was not to be trifled with!

MOON FACT FILE

- The Moon is 238,887 mi (384,401 km) from the Earth.

- The Moon reflects one four-hundred-and-twenty-five-thousandth of the Sun's brightness. (The Sun is the only thing in the Solar System that makes light.)

- The surface temperature of the Moon is between −247 °F (−155 °C) and 221 °F (105 °C)!

- The time between one new Moon and the next is 29 days, 12 hours, and 44 minutes.

- The Moon's *craters* (bowl-shaped holes) were formed between 3.5 and 4.5 billion years ago by *meteorites* (space rocks) hitting the surface.

- The same side of the Moon always faces the Earth. It wasn't until the Russian *probe* (vehicle that explores space) *Luna 3* sent back photographs of the far side in 1959 that it was seen for the first time.

- The Moon is the Earth's only *satellite* (object that moves around another one). It is about a quarter of the Earth's size.

- The Moon is 4.6 billion years old!

- In 1950, the Moon seemed to turn blue because a huge forest fire in Canada sent up clouds of smoke particles!

MAN ON THE MOON

On July 20, 1969, the Americans landed their *Apollo 11* spacecraft (right) on the Moon. The astronaut Neil Armstrong became the first person to set foot on the Moon's surface.

SET IN TIME

The Moon's surface has no air and no water, so the footprints left by the first astronauts will remain imprinted for millions of years.

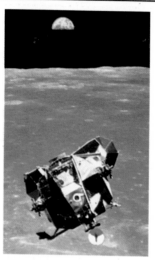

Astronaut's footprint

BELIEVE IT OR NOT...

If the *Apollo 11* astronauts had been "driving" only 1 mph (1.6 kph) too fast, they would have missed the Moon by 1,000 mi (1,600 km)!

EARLY ASTRONOMERS

The word *astronomy* comes from Greek words meaning "to name the stars." The Greeks were the first people to catalog the stars, although others had been studying them for thousands of years before.

AN EYE ON THE SKY

The earliest astronomers were probably farmers and shepherds who watched the skies for signs of changing weather and shifts in the seasons.

AZTECS AND INCAS

Two ancient peoples called the Aztecs and the Incas worshiped the Sun. The Inca kings even believed that they were descended from the Sun god, Inti! They believed in many myths about the stars.

Inca image of the sky or Moon god

EARLIEST RECORDS

The earliest astronomical records are clay tablets from a place called Mesopotamia. The calculations were based on years and years of observation.

Early astronomical records

GOLDEN CALCULATOR

The calculations required to figure out the positions of the planets and the stars are very, very complicated. Ancient astronomers used an instrument called an *astrolabe,* which was engraved with a flat reproduction of the heavens.

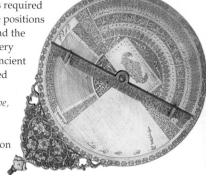

FARTHER INTO SPACE

Today, astronomers have really complicated instruments to bring us staggering information about our Universe. In 1990, the *Hubble Space Telescope* (below) was launched and is now sending back excellent images of things several billion light-years away.

THE WORLD OF STARS

When you look at the stars on a clear night, you are only seeing about 3,000 of the billion stars in our galaxy. They look tiny, but they are really ENORMOUS!

THE CONSTELLATIONS

The patterns and shapes that the stars make in the sky are called constellations. The top half of the world, called the *northern hemisphere*, sees different constellations from the bottom half, called the *southern hemisphere*.

Northern hemisphere star map

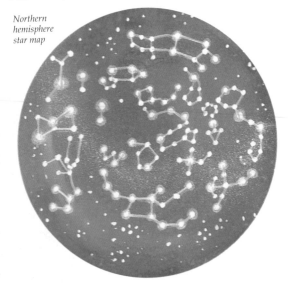

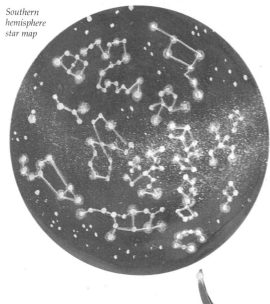

Southern hemisphere star map

STARS AND MYTHOLOGY

Astronomers group the stars into 88 constellations, each of which has a Latin name and is meant to represent a person or creature from ancient mythology.

Pattern of stars representing a bull ———

BELIEVE IT OR NOT...

It would take 4.2 light-years for light to reach Earth from the nearest star, Proxima Centauri.

STARGAZING

Since at least 2000 BC, people have known that curved glass can magnify things. In the 13th and 14th centuries, the Europeans used lenses to help improve poor sight. In the 17th century, telescopes appeared and people began serious stargazing.

MIGHTY MAGNIFIERS

The earliest telescopes were cumbersome affairs. The technology did not exist to make large lenses, so the only solution was to make very long telescopes, which helped magnification.

7-ft (2.1-m) long telescope

Today, multimirror telescopes focus on the sky. This telescope (left) in Arizona is made up of six separate mirrors, each measuring 6 ft (1.8 m) in diameter. Now that's big!

CAUGHT ON CAMERA

Before the invention of photography, astronomers had to draw everything that they saw through the telescope. Once the camera came along, astronomers could take photographs of the stars instead.

WATCHING IN COMFORT

In early times, astronomers worked out in the open, so they often got rather wet!

Now, astronomers watch the skies from observatories with dome-shaped roofs.

Some of the greatest early observatories were in the Middle East. The one below was built at Jaipur in Rajasthan, India, in 1726.

SAILING IN THE DARK

The earliest sailors only had the stars to navigate by. They had no real idea of where they were going or what they would find at the end of their journey.

Later, once sailors understood the movements of the stars and planets, and the relationship between angles and distances, they devised a more accurate system for finding their way around the oceans.

THEIR NAMES IN STARS

The sky we see at night has changed very little from the sky observed by the earliest astronomers. They would often have seen more clearly with the naked eye than we can now because of pollution and the glare of our streetlights.

CLAUDIUS PTOLEMAEUS (AROUND AD 100-178)

Known as Ptolemy, he was the source of all that we know about ancient astronomy. He collected the work of the astronomers who had lived before him and his two important books were the leading authority for 1,600 years!

NICOLAUS COPERNICUS (1473-1543)

He died the year that he published a book that changed everyone's ideas about the Universe. He was one of a number of astronomers who said that the Sun, not the Earth, was the center of the Universe.

GALILEO GALILEI (1564-1642)

Galileo was a brilliant astronomer who had the great misfortune of being born at a time when brilliant scientific thinking was considered dangerous. He was sentenced to what was virtually life imprisonment and was finally pardoned in 1992! A little on the late side!

TYCHO BRAHE (1546-1601)

He produced the first complete star atlas by remeasuring the 788 stars in Ptolemy's catalog. He built a huge observatory (right) near Copenhagen in Denmark to continue his studies.

ISAAC NEWTON (1642-1727)

He was born the year that Galileo died. He invented the first reflecting telescope, which got a much better quality image than earlier telescopes. He also laid out the rules of *gravity* (the pulling force that attracts objects to one another) after watching apples fall off a tree in the garden!

EDMOND HALLEY (1656-1742)

He noticed that there had been three very similar descriptions of a comet recorded every 76 years, and he predicted that it would return in 1758. He was right, but he didn't live to take the credit. The comet, which now bears his name, last returned in 1986.

Halley's comet

TIMEKEEPING

The Earth takes one full day and one full night to spin once on its axis. This period of time is divided into 24 hours; each hour is divided into 60 minutes; each minute is divided into 60 seconds. A year is based on the time it takes the Earth to go around the Sun.

Sandglass

CLOCK STARS
The ancient Egyptians used 36 "clock stars" to tell the time at night. They used an instrument called a *merkhet* to observe the movement of certain stars, so they could figure out the hours.

SAND CLOCKS
In the Middle Ages, around AD 1300, the *sandglass* was used to measure the passing of time. The modern equivalent of this is an egg timer! Very down-to-earth!

SUN CLOCKS
Clocks that use the Sun to tell the time are called *sundials*. The shadow cast by the upright of the sundial falls onto a series of markers. Sundials were used frequently in the past. Some were huge buildings while others were small enough to fit into a pocket.

Folding sundial

TIME AROUND THE WORLD

Because different parts of the Earth face the Sun at different times, their nights and days are different. For instance, when it is midday in London, England, it is nighttime in Sydney, Australia, so all the people in the world have to set their clocks to different times. The Earth is divided into 24 *time zones*, one for every hour of the day.

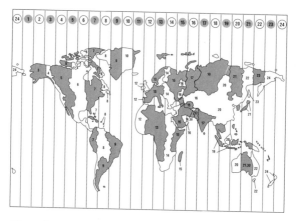

Throughout each zone, the time is the same, but if you cross to the next zone you have to change your watch – put it back an hour going west or forward an hour going east.

DARK AND LIGHT

The polar lands, the Arctic and the Antarctic, can be unfriendly places – cold, windy, and dark. In the winter, the Sun doesn't shine at all since it never rises above the horizon. Brrrr!

THE LAND OF THE MIDNIGHT SUN

Any land north of the Arctic Circle is called the Land of the Midnight Sun. In the summer, the Sun hardly ever sinks below the horizon and it seems to be day all day and all night! In the winter, the reverse happens and it is almost completely dark all the time.

WHITEOUT

The weather condition called a *whiteout* is a real hazard in the Arctic. It seems to happen mostly in the summer when the light comes from all around, and there are no shadows. It becomes impossible to get your bearings and you just have to wait until the weather changes!

WINTER PASTIMES

The Inuit people (or Eskimos) who live in the Arctic are very restricted in their winter activities. There is very little light, so they can't hunt much. Instead, they spend their time carving wood, bone, and walrus tusks into beautiful statues of animals, birds, and hunting scenes.

SPECIAL EFFECTS

Sometimes, on cold winter nights, the Moon appears to have a halo around it. This is caused by ice crystals high up in the Earth's *atmosphere* (the layer of gases around the planet). They bend the sunlight that is reflected toward Earth by the Moon.

Very rarely, you might see a *moonbow*, which is the very faint nighttime equivalent of a daytime rainbow.

GLORIOUS LIGHTS

The *aurora borealis* is a spectacular display of light in the night sky. It is caused by particles from the Sun striking gases in the atmosphere high above the North Pole.

Aurora borealis

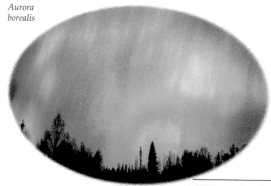

SEEING IN THE DARK

There have been endless inventions to make nighttime vision easier: Some are sensible and some are very bizarre!

CAT'S EYES
An Englishman, Percy Shaw, invented a road safety device to help guide motorists driving at night. After being saved from crashing on a foggy road by the reflection from the eyes of a cat, he came up with an invention to go in the middle of the road...*cat's eyes*, of course! Clever, huh?

Beads reflect light from car headlights

LIGHTING THE WAY
Driving at night in the days of early automobiles was hazardous! In the daytime, a man walked in front of the car with a red flag to warn pedestrians and to make drivers keep their speed down. At night he couldn't be seen, so an oil lamp was carried. Electric lights became standard fixtures on cars in the 1930s.

DOWN THE LINE

A *laser beam* is a special, intense beam of light that has many different uses. It measures distances, scans goods in the supermarket, and is used in compact disc players.

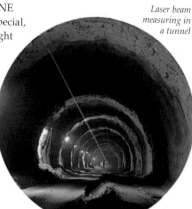

Laser beam measuring in a tunnel

NIGHT VISION

Soldiers can now use special binoculars that give them enough night vision to see people and equipment moving in the dark.

INSIDE OUT

Surgeons can use an instrument called an *endoscope* to see inside your body. Light travels along lots of *fiber-optic* wires to the tip of the instrument and lights up the darkness. The operator looks into the eyepiece to see inside.

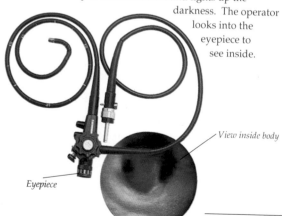

View inside body

Eyepiece

LIGHT FANTASTIC

In ancient times, people used to worship the Sun because their lives depended on it rising every day to give warmth and help plants grow. Here are some light facts to brighten dark evenings.

MAN OF MANY PARTS

Leonardo da Vinci (1452-1519) was an artist, engineer, and scientist, and he left lots of notes on all his investigations, including the study of light. In many of his paintings, he used light and dark to give a dramatic effect.

PROFILE IN BLACK

Étienne de Silhouette (1709-1767) gave his name to the technique of using shadow images to create pictures. He originally used the idea to make portraits of people that were much cheaper than oil paintings.

STRAIGHT LINES

Light travels in straight lines. You can see this if a shaft of sunlight comes through a window and lights up dust or water in the air.

Sunbeam shows light travels in straight lines.

ENERGETIC
The Sun produces a huge amount of energy every day. In a sunny spot, it can generate 2,000 kilowatt-hours of light energy in a year. This would be enough to boil a tea kettle nonstop for six weeks!

GONE IN A FLASH
The first person to attempt to record the speed of light was a Danish astronomer called Olaus Roemer, in 1675. It wasn't until Léon Foucault (1819-1868) did some experiments in the 1800s that people realized that the speed of light varied depending on what it was traveling through – water or glass for instance.

FACE THE LIGHT
Plants grow toward the light since they need the Sun's energy to survive and grow. The French name for the sunflower is *tournesol*, which means "turn toward the Sun."

LIGHTS AND LAMPS

Greek legend says that the god Zeus didn't want humans to have fire, but Prometheus stole it and brought it down to Earth. We commemorate this at the beginning of the Olympic Games, when runners bring a flame from Greece to the stadium.

FIRE! FIRE!

Fire was vital to early people for keeping warm, frightening off wild animals, roasting meat, and hardening spear tips. At first, they probably used accidental fires caused by lightning. Then they discovered that they could make sparks by hitting two stones together or by rubbing two sticks together.

OIL POWER

Early people realized that the oil from the animals they ate would give out light if it caught fire. The next step was to put some of this oil into a shallow stone to create a primitive lamp.

*Roman clay oil lamp
with covered top*

CANDLES

The first ever candles were made over 2,000 years ago, but they were too expensive for most people. Oil from animals was boiled down to make tallow, which was poured over a wick and left to cool.

Beeswax sheets can be rolled around a wick to make candles. Beeswax candles give off a nice fragrance when burned.

IDEAL MATCH

A short wooden stick, otherwise known as a match, was a marvelous invention. It was tipped with a mixture of chemicals that caught fire if the match was struck against a rough surface.

Matches and candle

Rough surface

ALL LIT UP

After oil lamps, gas was used to provide light. In the 19th century, towns and cities were lit by jets of burning gas. Sounds dangerous!

If you're wondering about electricity, then turn the page!

What Electricity Can Do

There has always been electricity in our world. Skies can be lit up by lightning (natural electricity), and there are animals that can make electricity. Scientists have gradually harnessed electrical energy, which we now use in countless ways.

Glow in the Dark

In about 1880, Thomas Edison and Joseph Swan invented the lightbulb at almost the same time, without each other knowing. The light comes from a very thin wire called a *carbon filament*, suspended in a glass bulb.

Carbon filament

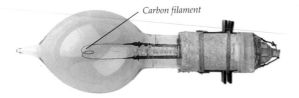

The Flick of a Switch

In the 1880s, big cities like New York, London, and Paris became the first to use electricity for lighting. However, it was years before enough cables were laid to make electric light easily available.

BELIEVE IT OR NOT...

In the early days, electric light seemed miraculous. Many people were deeply suspicious of electricity and worried that it might "seep out" of the sockets!

COLORFUL

Today, there are different kinds of lightbulbs for various uses. A *daylight bulb* creates natural daylight. The light comes from a mixture of colors, just like sunlight, and is excellent for doing close work. *Sodium lamps* are often used for lighting cities. They give off a yellow light.

NO STARS TO BE SEEN

As with most technical advances, there is a downside to all this light. Light pollution is now a real problem. In some cities, people are not able to see the stars, and the sky always looks bright and yellow at night, not black.

NIGHT LIFE

Some animals are *nocturnal*. This means that they come out at night and sleep during the day.

HEDGEHOGS

Most hedgehogs rest during the day and come out at night to hunt for earthworms and insects. They have sensitive whiskers that help them find their way around.

In northern parts of the world, hedgehogs *hibernate* (sleep all winter), curled up in a tight ball, and only come out when spring arrives.

Curled up

On the move

MOLES

Moles are underground creatures with very poor eyesight but excellent hearing. They dig elaborate tunnels below ground, throwing the leftover soil up to the surface where it forms molehills. Moles mainly live on worms. Yum, yum!

SHREWS

Shrews look like mice but have longer noses and tiny eyes. The smaller ones have to eat their own weight in food every 24 hours to survive! They have to hunt during the night and day to get enough to eat!

SLUGS

Slugs eat almost everything green in sight, but they in turn make a very tasty meal for hedgehogs! They mostly slime their way around at night since they need to keep damp, and sunshine would dry them out. Most mini-beasts prefer to move around in the dark.

FROGS

Frogs prefer nighttime foraging. Males do a lot of croaking at night to attract females!

WORMS

Earthworms come to the surface at night to grab leaves to munch on in the safety of their tunnels during the day. They also come out in the day if it is wet. A ready-made meal for a hungry bird!

NIGHT BIRDS

Some birds are only seen, or even just heard, at nighttime.

NIGHT TRAVELERS

Almost half of the world's birds *migrate* (fly to another country) each year to find good weather, food and water, and to nest. They use landmarks, the Sun, the Moon, and the stars to find their way. Many travel night and day without food or sleep.

SECRETIVE SONGSTER

The nightingale is a shy bird that nests in thick shrubs and low bushes. It sings during the day, but its glorious voice is best heard at night when all the other birds are asleep. It is a plain little bird to look at, but its song is rich and varied, full of trills and warbles.

FROG KEBAB

The night heron is often seen standing on one leg by a riverbank, absolutely motionless, until it makes a sudden jab and skewers a frog on the end of its beak. Ouch!

Night heron

HIDDEN FROM VIEW

The nightjar eats at dusk when the air is full of insects. During the daytime it stays in its nest, amazingly camouflaged to look just like a broken twig or branch.

Spot the nightjar!

NOISY CHORUS

Starlings have become a great menace in some cities. Thousands of them fly in great flocks at dusk to find places to roost overnight. There have been different plans to discourage them, including bright lights, but the lights warm up the cold stone of the buildings where they perch, turning it into comfy underground heating!

Starling

TOO-WHIT, TOO-WHOO!

Owls are very rarely seen during the day since most of them are nighttime hunters. They are powerful and silent as they swoop down on unsuspecting prey.

SHARP EYES
Most birds of prey have *binocular vision*, which means that both eyes point directly to the front, giving very accurate sight.

Their eyes cannot turn very far in their sockets, but an owl can turn its whole head right around and look to the back. Yikes!

ODD EARS
Owls have excellent hearing. They can hear the slightest rustle in the undergrowth from an unwary mouse. Some owls have tufts on their heads that look like ears, but these are only feathers.

Eurasian eagle owl

SILENT KILLER

The owl has very soft, fluffy feathers, a small body, and big wings so it can swoop down almost noiselessly onto its prey. It catches and kills its victims with its sharp claws, called *talons*.

LEFTOVERS

Because owls don't have teeth, they eat everything whole. They have to cough up fur, beaks, feet, bones, and feathers in a lump called a pellet. Gross!

WHAT A HOOT!

People used to think that an owl's cry came from evil spirits! This sound actually warns other birds to keep away from the owl's territory, but it can sound very eerie on a dark night.

THE SECRETIVE BADGER

Badgers are nocturnal creatures that live in family groups. Their favorite times are dawn and dusk, when the younger ones love to romp and play.

BADGER PORTRAIT

Badgers are stout, heavy animals, with short, thick legs and heavy fur coats. They have strong claws to help them dig. Although they have small eyes and poor eyesight, they have an excellent sense of smell – ideal for hunting out large quantities of earthworms, small animals, fruit, and nuts. They can produce a very unpleasant smell to deter their enemies, just like their relatives, skunks.

HAPPY FAMILIES

Each badger family may have as many as fifteen members. There are usually two or three babies, called *cubs*, which are born in the spring.

HOME SWEET HOME

Badgers live in an underground home called a *set*, made up of an elaborate system of tunnels and chambers. Some sets are over 100 years old and have been used by generations of badgers. The set has many ways in and out, and the badgers keep it very clean. They bring in fresh grass, leaves, and moss to make up beds in the larger chambers.

A set can have more than 20 entrances and house up to 15 badgers

PERSONAL ID

Badgers have distinctive stripes on their faces. These stripes are useful camouflage when they are stomping through the undergrowth. No two sets of stripes are the same, so they may also help the animals recognize each other.

BATS

Bats are the only flying *mammals* (animals that give birth to live young, which they feed with their own milk). There are tiny bats, smaller than butterflies, and others with a wingspan as wide as the height of an adult. All bats are nighttime creatures.

ECHO SOUNDER

Bats find their way around in the dark by *echolocation*. This means that they squeak as they fly and the sound bounces off anything in the way. The bat can hear the echo with its huge ears and can judge what the object is, what size it is, and where it is, all within a split second! That's a pretty nifty hunting device.

A bat's wings need to be kept in good condition for flying.

DAY NURSERIES

Female bats all have their babies at the same time. For a few months they set up nurseries in the caves where they live, and look after all the babies together. The babies can fly within four months.

FRUIT CASE

The largest bat in the world is the fruit bat, sometimes called the flying fox because of its foxy-looking face. Fruit bats are huge – as much as 5 ft 6 in (1.7 m) from wing tip to wing tip! They fly out at dawn and dusk to feed on fruit, flowers, and leaves.

Fruit bat

BELIEVE IT OR NOT...
The tiniest bat is called Kitti's hognosed bat. It is about 1 in (3 cm) long.

UPSIDE-DOWN DREAMS

Bats sleep upside down. They don't have a very powerful grip with their hands, but they can hang on with their feet. They often sleep together in great numbers.

BLOODTHIRSTY

The vampire bat (left) comes out at night in search of animal and bird blood! It is the size of a small mouse and has two very sharp, pointed teeth that can inject *saliva* (spit) into the victim's blood to stop it from *clotting* (going thick and lumpy). The bat then slurps up the flowing blood. Gross!

MOTHS

Some moths are seen during the day, but they are mostly night flyers. They have fur on their bodies to keep them warm.

BEAUTIFUL MOTHS

There are at least 150,000 different kinds of moths compared to only 15,000 butterflies. Not all moths are drab and dull – some are as gaudy as butterflies, especially those that live in tropical regions.

Exotic moths

DAYTIME CAMOUFLAGE

Moths hide during the day to escape *predators* (hunters) such as bats. Some have colors that help them "disappear" against their chosen background. Others frighten predators away by looking fierce, often with fake eyes on the backs of their wings.

Startling eye spot

MONSTER MOTH

The atlas moth is among the biggest moths in the world – even bigger than many birds! Its wingspan can be as great as 12 in (30 cm) and even the caterpillars are twice as long as your middle finger!

Atlas moth

MOTH EARS

Some moths can escape from bats since they have eardrums that can pick up the bats' squeaks. The moth can then duck and dive, or rest on the ground until the danger has passed. Phew!

TOO BRIGHT

Moths are attracted to bright lights and this is one way that they can be captured for study. They can't tell the difference between candles and electric lightbulbs, though, so their curiosity can be fatal.

DESERTS BY NIGHT

Deserts are very hot by day and bitterly cold at night. Desert animals have adapted themselves to their harsh surroundings. Many rest during the day to avoid the heat and emerge at night.

HOT, HOT, HOT!

The ground gecko finds the hot desert sand very uncomfortable. It mainly comes out at night to avoid the problem.

Ground gecko

A HUGE SWARM

Locusts are grasshoppers that can cause incredible damage to crops. A swarm of locusts can devour 22,050 tons (20,000 tonnes) of plants in a day. They have been known to fly in such huge swarms, millions at a time, that they blot out the Sun! They rest during the heat of the day but can travel as far as about $^1/_2$ mile (1 km) during an evening.

Locust

STING IN THE TAIL

The scorpion is one of the deadliest desert creatures. It uses its sting to kill prey and some have a sting strong enough to kill a person. Don't panic, though; scorpions only do this if they are threatened or stepped on by accident!

During the day, scorpions hide under stones. They can survive without water because they get enough moisture from their food.

SSSSSSNAKES

Most desert snakes hide in sandy burrows during the day and come out to hunt at night. The desert kingsnake has slit-shaped pupils in its eyes that can open wide to help it see better in the dark.

Rattlesnakes warn off their enemies by rattling the hollow segments at the end of their tails.

Rattle

Rattlesnake

ADAPTABLE NATURE

Here are some more nocturnal animals that have developed ways of coping with their nighttime existence.

BIG EARS

The fennec fox lives in the desert. It is the smallest member of the fox family at only 16 in (40 cm) from nose to tail. Its HUGE ears give off body heat and cool the fox down.

The fox stays in its burrow during the day and hunts lizards and desert creatures called jerboas at night.

Desert hedgehogs have big ears, too!

Big ears give off heat.

BLACK HUNTER

A panther is a black leopard. It prowls unseen through the forest at night, hunting for food. In the day, it rests in tree branches.

FURRY FEET

Gerbils live in burrows during the day but become very active at night. They have fur on the undersides of their feet to protect them from the burning heat of the desert sand.

SPINY MICE

Spiny mice come out at night. They have a handy secret weapon! If an enemy grabs a spiny mouse by the tail, that is all it will get! The mouse simply sheds its tail and scuttles off. Wow!

GLOW IN THE DARK

Many animals, fish, and plants can glow in the dark...and that's without the aid of a flashlight!

GLOWING FISH

Many deep-sea fish, such as lantern fish and angler fish, glow in the dark. Their light is made to send out signals to other fish – predators beware, and mates are attracted!

Angler fish   *This part glows.*

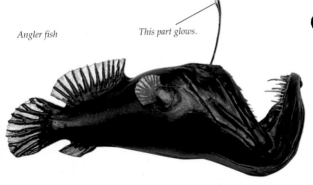

The viper fish is a horrible-looking creature that puts out a glow from its dorsal fin (back fin) and then impales its victim on its big fangs.

Viper fish and victim

WARNING FLASH

Flashlight fish have big lights beneath their eyes that they can flash on and off to warn the rest of the school of any approaching danger.

GLOWING TOADSTOOLS

Plant life can glow, too! Some fungi glow in the dark and can be seen as far away as 44 yds (40 m).

FIREFLIES

When thousands of fireflies swarm at night, the skies are all lit up. Each firefly has an amazingly bright glow that is used as a communication signal. Most fireflies are tropical, but there are some European and North American varieties.

GLOWING WATER

Sometimes the sea looks as if it is on fire! This is caused by very tiny sea creatures called *plankton* that flash as the water is churned up by passing ships or the waves.

Plankton

NIGHT FRIGHTS

People have always found nighttime frightening. In earliest times, they were fearful that the Sun wouldn't rise again, and many myths arose to explain the strange sounds and sights that could be heard. The superstitious could easily persuade people that witches and ghosts were present!

HOWLING WOLF

Wolves howling at night is a chilling sound, but they won't attack humans unless provoked. They howl to communicate with each other.

FACT OR FICTION?

People used to believe that the lights seen over marshland were from evil goblins, leading unwary travelers to their doom. The truth is not as dramatic as this! The light occurs naturally, from the gases produced by rotting *vegetation* (plant life).

COUNT DRACULA

The human vampire Count Dracula, who lives off the blood of the innocent, is entirely the invention of the Irish writer Bram Stoker, who wrote his classic horror story in 1897.

WITCHES AND WARLOCKS

For hundreds of years, people believed in witches who had evil and strange powers. Women branded as witches were probably early healers, who used herbs and common sense to cure many everyday ailments, and not evil at all!

BLACK CATS

Superstitious people say that black cats are the companions of witches. They are alleged to have supernatural powers for both good and evil. So treat your kitty with respect!

INDEX

America 7, 12
Armstrong, Neil 7
astronomy 4, 8, 9, 11-15
aurora borealis 19
Aztecs 8

badger 34, 35
bats 36, 37
Big Bang 2
birds 30, 31, 32, 33

candles 25
cat's eyes 20
Chinese 4
Christopher Columbus 5
comet 15
constellations 11

deserts 40, 41

Earth 2-6, 16, 17, 19
eclipses 5
Egyptians (ancient) 16
electricity 26, 27

fire 24
fireflies 45
fish 44
fox 42
frogs 29

gas 25
gerbils 43
glowing toadstools 45
Greeks 8, 24

hedgehogs 28

Incas 8
light 3, 10, 19-27
locusts 40

matches 25
Mexicans 4
mice 43
moles 28
Moon 4, 5, 6, 7, 19
moths 38, 39

nightingale 30
nightjar 31

oil 24, 25
owls 32, 33

planets 2, 9, 13

radar 21

sandfish 40
scorpion 41
shrews 29
slugs 29
snakes 41
starlings 31
stars 8-14, 16
Sun 2, 3, 5, 6, 8, 14, 16-19, 22, 23

telescopes 9, 12, 15
timekeeping 16, 17

wolves 46
worms 29

Acknowledgments: (KEY: a=above, b=bottom/below, c=center, l=left, r=right, t=top) National Maritime Museum, Greenwich, London; Natural History Museum; Noordwijk Space Expo; Science Museum, London.

Picture Credits: Allsport/Vandystadt: 24tl; Ancient Art & Architecture Collection: 8bl; Ardea/Adrian Warren: 37bl; EN Arnold: 40c; Bruce Coleman Inc.: 45cr; Bruce Coleman Ltd./Rod Williams: 42b; Ken Day: 22b; Mary Evans Picture Library: 15t; John Hawkins/Eric & David Hosking: 33; Michael Holford: 8cr; Frank Lane Picture Agency/Eric & David Hosking: 29t; NASA: 6; 7tr; 7b; /JPL: front cover tl; National Optical Astro Observatory: 15b; NHPA/JH Carmichael: 45br; /Stephen Dalton: 28br; Oxford Scientific Films/Animals, Animals: 45cl; Planet Earth Pictures/John Eastcott: 30c; /Norbert Wu: 44b; Science Photo Library: 14cr; 19b; /Dr. Fred Espenak: 5; /NASA: 9b; /Pekka Parviainen: 19c; /R. Ressmeyer, 27b; /R. Ressmeyer, Starlight: 12clb; Tony Stone Images: 26tr; Wild Images/Dutcher Film Productions: 46; Zefa Pictures: 10tl; /Bramaz: 21t; /Gunter Heil: 13.

Additional Photography: Jane Burton, Peter Chadwick, Tina Chambers, Frank Greenaway, Colin Keates, Dave King, Cyril Laubscher, Jerry Young.

Additional Illustrations: Janos Marffy, Daniel J. Pyne.